Oceanography and Hydrology

THE STUDY OF SCIENCE

Oceanography and Hydrology

Edited by Nicholas Croce

Britannica®
Educational Publishing

IN ASSOCIATION WITH

ROSEN
EDUCATIONAL SERVICES

Published in 2017 by Britannica Educational Publishing (a trademark of Encyclopædia Britannica, Inc.) in association with The Rosen Publishing Group, Inc.
29 East 21st Street, New York, NY 10010

Distributed exclusively by Rosen Publishing.
To see additional Britannica Educational Publishing titles, go to rosenpublishing.com.

First Edition

Britannica Educational Publishing
J.E. Luebering: Executive Editor, Core Editorial
Anthony L. Green: Editor, Compton's by Britannica

Rosen Publishing
Nicholas Croce: Editor
Nelson Sá: Art Director
Brian Garvey: Designer
Cindy Reiman: Photography Manager
Cindy Reiman: Photo Researcher

Library of Congress Cataloging-in-Publication Data

Names: Croce, Nicholas.
Title: Oceanography and hydrology / edited by Nicholas Croce.
Description: New York : Britannica Educational Publishing, [2016] | Series:
 The Study of Science | Includes bibliographical references and index.
Identifiers: LCCN 2015034556 | ISBN 9781680482355 (library bound : alk. paper)
Subjects: LCSH: Oceanography--Juvenile literature. | Hydrology--Juvenile
 literature.
Classification: LCC GC21.5 .O29 2016 | DDC 551.46--dc23
LC record available at http://lccn.loc.gov/2015034556

Manufactured in China

CONTENTS

CONTENTS

Water close to Earth's surface, such as the Epupa Falls in Namibia, is essential for life.

Nearly three-fourths of Earth's surface is covered with water. Perhaps the most important liquid in the world, water is usually easy to get from rain, springs, wells, streams, rivers, ponds, and lakes. It fills the vast ocean beds. As vapor, water is also present in the air, where it often condenses into clouds. As ice, it forms vast glaciers and polar ice caps. Water is essential for life. It is the most critical nutrient for all living things and plays a key role in many natural processes. Bodies of water, from the smallest pond to the largest sea, provide habitat for a myriad of organisms.

Oceanography is the scientific study of all aspects of the oceans, their boundaries, and their contents. The major branches of this study are concerned with the physical nature of the oceans, their chemical and mineral constituents, the great variety of living things that inhabit the

oceans, and the geological structure of the ocean floor. Oceanography is also concerned with the technical and economic potentials of the oceans.

Hydrology, in its widest sense, encompasses the study of the movement and characteristics of water in all its forms within the hydrosphere, the part of Earth that includes all the liquid water on, just below, and just above the planet's surface. Water in the atmosphere is usually studied as part of meteorology. Water in the oceans and seas is studied within oceanography. The study of the water in lakes and inland seas is called limnology; the study of ice on Earth's landmasses is the concern of glaciology. There is some overlap among these disciplines—for example, both hydrologists and meteorologists may study the movement of water in the lower atmosphere—but all are linked by the fundamental concept of the water cycle.

The water cycle involves the circulation of water in all of its forms. Sun, air, water, and the force of gravity work together to keep the water cycle going. Major steps in the cycle include: the evaporation of water by the Sun's heat and the transpiration of water by plants; the condensation of water vapor by cold air; the precipitation of water by gravity; and the

return of water by gravity to the oceans. Some water evaporates into the air from rivers, lakes, moist soil, and plants, but most of the water that moves over Earth's surface comes from, and eventually returns to, the oceans.

Through the processes of the water cycle, Earth's water constantly circulates through the hydrosphere. The timescale of this cycle is vast—a person taking a drink of water today may be drinking the same water that gave refreshment to humans living thousands of years ago. Although water constantly cycles through the hydrosphere, many areas of Earth have a scarce supply.

Although all water is important, it is freshwater that is needed to sustain life. Most of Earth's water—roughly 97.5 percent—is salt water and is found mainly in the oceans and seas. The remaining 2.5 percent of Earth's water is freshwater—however, most of that (about 68.6 percent) is frozen in polar ice caps and glaciers or locked up below Earth's surface as groundwater (about 30.1 percent). Only about 1.3 percent of Earth's freshwater is surface water, the water readily available for use by living things. Developments in the fields of oceanography and hydrology have helped people make responsible use of the critical resource of freshwater.

CHAPTER 1

STUDY OF THE OCEANS AND THE SEAS

E arth is the only one of the eight planets in the solar system that is known to have an appreciable amount of water on its surface. About 71 percent of Earth's surface is covered by the oceans, and half of the world is covered by a layer of water more than two miles in depth. More than 97 percent of the water on Earth is in the oceans.

Oceanography is concerned with all aspects of Earth's oceans and seas. The field is subdivided into several specialized areas of study. Physical oceanography is the study of the properties of seawater, including the formation of sea ice, the movement of seawater through waves, currents, and tides, and the interactions between the oceans and the atmosphere. Chemical oceanography is concerned with the composition of seawater and the physical, biological, and chemical processes that govern changes in composition in time and space. Marine geology deals with the geologic evolution of

All of Earth's oceans are part of one global body of water—the world ocean.

the ocean basins, while biological oceanography (also called marine ecology) focuses on the living things that inhabit the sea.

The great body of water embracing Earth's continents may be viewed as one vast entity—the world ocean. Its major subdivisions are the Pacific, the Atlantic, the Indian, and the Arctic Oceans. Some people further divide the world ocean into the North Pacific, South Pacific, North Atlantic, South Atlantic, Indian, Arctic, and Antarctic (or Southern) Oceans, for a total of seven. This should not be confused,

however, with the popular term "seven seas," which originated with medieval Arabic geographers who knew only the waters of Europe and Asia.

Around the borders of the oceans lie partially enclosed seas and gulfs, such as the Mediterranean, Caribbean, Baltic, Black, Red, and North Seas, the Gulf of Mexico, and the Persian Gulf. The landlocked Caspian Sea was part of a great ocean in an earlier geologic era. Gulfs are generally described as extensions of oceans or seas. The Gulf of Mexico is larger than most seas. In addition to seas and gulfs are straits, narrow marine passageways connecting two large bodies of water. The Strait of Gibraltar, which connects the Atlantic Ocean and the Mediterranean Sea, is an example.

The Atlantic, Pacific, Indian, and Arctic Oceans cover approximately 129,428,700 square miles (335,218,800 square kilometers). The Pacific Ocean is the largest, occupying almost one-third of Earth's total area. The oceans are not evenly distributed over Earth's surface. About 43 percent of their total area lies in the Northern Hemisphere and 57 percent in the Southern Hemisphere.

The word *ocean* is derived from Oceanus — in Greek mythology one of the Titans. He was a son of Uranus (the sky) and Gaea (Earth), the first rulers of the world. Oceanus personified the river that the Greeks believed encircled the flat Earth.

The oceans influenced the formation of Earth's land surface as it is known today. During several periods of Earth's history large parts of North America were covered by the ocean. Most of the limestone, sandstone, and shale on land was deposited as sediment on the bottom of ancient, shallow seas. Chalk, such as that found in England, Texas, and Kansas, was formed on seabeds from the shells of sea creatures.

Climate and weather patterns are profoundly influenced by the oceans. Water has a high capacity for storing heat. It warms more slowly than land, and it also cools more slowly. Thus the coasts of the continents have cooler summers and warmer winters than the inland areas. One example of this moderating effect is the Gulf Stream, a warm ocean current in the North Atlantic. The Gulf Stream carries warm water from the Gulf of Mexico northeast along the North American coast and then eastward toward the shores of Europe. This helps keep winter air temperatures in Norway and southwestern England relatively warmer than the average for inland areas at the same latitude.

The oceans are also the birthplace of storms that affect climate throughout the world.

THE ORIGIN OF THE OCEAN BASINS

The development and location of the present ocean basins can be explained by plate tectonics, an overarching theory that explains the motions of Earth's outer layers. According to the theory, Earth has a rigid outer layer, known as the lithosphere, that overlies a softer layer of molten rock called the asthenosphere. The lithosphere is broken up into about a dozen large plates and several small ones. These plates move relative to each other, typically at rates of 2 to 4 inches (5 to 10 centimeters) per year.

Most scientists believe the development of the present ocean basins began some 200 million years ago with the breakup of Pangaea, an enormous landmass composed of nearly all the present-day continents. Over a long time, the landmasses that had comprised Pangaea drifted into new configurations as the plates carrying them moved across Earth's surface. These movements led to the shrinking of the Pacific Basin at the expense of the growing Atlantic and Arctic Basins, the opening and closing of seaways in the tropical latitudes, and the opening of the Southern Ocean as the southern continents moved north away from Antarctica.

The causes of plate motions are not completely understood. However, a major factor appears to be giant convection cells (churning motions) in the mantle, a thick layer of molten rock that includes the asthenosphere and extends toward Earth's core. Currents of hot material in the mantle rise while currents of colder material sink, forming roughly circular cells—the same pattern of heat circulation that can be seen in a pot of boiling water. This

The shape of Earth's oceans and seas has changed significantly throughout the past 600 million years.

circulation causes material to rise from the mantle, forming new lithosphere at structures called oceanic ridges. The rise of material in these areas helps push older material away from the ridges, a process known as seafloor spreading. Near the edges of continents some of the oceanic material sinks into the mantle. These areas are called subduction zones; they are associated with oceanic troughs, volcanic activity, and certain types of earthquakes.

MINERAL RESOURCES OF THE OCEANS

The oceans function as a very large sump, or reservoir—all the sediments and wastes of the continents pour into them. Many of the elements contained in ocean water are mined for commercial purposes. Sodium chloride, or common table salt, is frequently obtained from the oceans, as is magnesium, a light-weight metal.

Another source of minerals is the ocean floor. Phosphorite deposits, consisting mainly of calcium phosphate, cover parts of the ocean bottom. Diamonds, gold, tin, iron, and sulfur are mined from shallow-water deposits and beaches. Petroleum and natural gas are extracted from the continental shelf.

Manganese nodules cover much of the ocean basins. Formed by chemical precipitation around a nucleus such as a shark's tooth or a piece of volcanic ash, they consist primarily of alternating layers of manganese and iron oxides. Other minerals present in high but varying concentrations are copper, nickel, and cobalt.

OCEAN FRONTIERS

In 1870 science-fiction writer Jules Verne captivated a large reading audience with his novel *Twenty Thousand Leagues Under the Sea,* a story of ocean exploration in the submarine *Nautilus*, guided by the rather forbidding Captain Nemo. The popularity of the novel was due in great part to humankind's centuries-old fascination with the mysteries of the sea. Here was a watery wilderness, tempting but terribly difficult to explore. The legend of the lost colony of Atlantis is another story that has fascinated people because it represents overcoming the difficulties of planting a settlement of humans deep in the ocean.

In the 20th century those difficulties were slowly overcome as devices were invented to explore the seas and mine their riches. Ocean exploration achievements have included

manned descent to a depth of 35,800 feet (10,910 meters); a submerged circumnavigation of the world; transits beneath the North Pole and the Arctic ice cap; the discovery of a mountain range system some 50,000 miles (80,000 kilometers) long through all the world's oceans; and an undersea laboratory that allows scientists to live and work underwater for almost two weeks before returning to the surface.

EXPLORING THE OCEAN DEPTHS

Undersea exploration is undertaken for military, scientific, and economic reasons by governments and by private industry. The economic factor has become increasingly important as oil and gas firms have developed their own oceanographic fleets and specialized instruments. Mining the seabeds for other minerals—nickel, cobalt, manganese, zinc, silver, gold, and other metals—also has become a significant enterprise.

In the 20th and early 21st centuries scientists made great strides in exploring the oceans. In the 1930s the American naturalist-explorer Charles William Beebe, with the American engineer Otis Barton, developed a submersible that could withstand water pressures at 3,000 to 4,000 feet (900 to 1,200 meters) deep. The device, called a bathysphere, was a spherical steel vessel provided with portholes and lowered into the ocean by a cable attached to a ship. Aboard the bathysphere, Beebe and Barton conducted a series of dives off the Bermuda coast that enabled them to study undersea life as never before.

The development of deep-diving undersea craft accelerated in the 1950s. A 1952 expedition found a canyon in the Atlantic Ocean the size of the Mississippi River and its tributaries. Another expedition used scuba gear to enable the explorers to dive as deep as 300 feet (90 meters) below the ocean surface.

In 1960 the "bottom of the world" was reached when U.S. Navy Lieutenant Donald Walsh and Swiss scientist Jacques Piccard dived 35,800 feet (10,900 meters) to the bottom of the Mariana Trench southwest of Guam in the Pacific Ocean. Their descent was made in a bathyscaphe, a variation on the bathysphere. Unlike the bathysphere, which was unpowered and suspended from a surface cable, bathyscaphes are self-propelled submersibles suspended below a float.

In 1968 the U.S. National Science Foundation began the Deep Sea Drilling Project, using the

OCEAN FLOOR EXPLOITATION

Early attempts to establish a law of the sea resulted in several United Nations conferences on the law of the sea (UNCLOS). At UNCLOS I, held in Geneva, Switzerland, in 1958, delegates from 86 nations ratified four agreements concerning the continental shelf, the high seas, the territorial sea and adjacent zone, and fishing and conservation of the living resources of the high seas.

Some of the issues addressed in the agreements involved the definition of territories such as the continental shelf. Many delineation rules were challenged. Of the 300 potential territorial-sea or continental-shelf boundaries, less than 25 percent of the boundaries were negotiated within 30 years of the original agreement. The rest were in dispute, in some stage of negotiation, or not being discussed. The majority of the boundaries divide the continental shelf of adjacent countries.

The United States was the first country to bring natural resources of the continental shelf under national jurisdiction and control. Many international lawyers contend, however, that such jurisdiction does not include the power to restrict navigation, fishing, or scientific inquiry. The deep-sea bed lies beyond the continental shelf. This vast region cannot be claimed by any nation and its legal status remains uncertain.

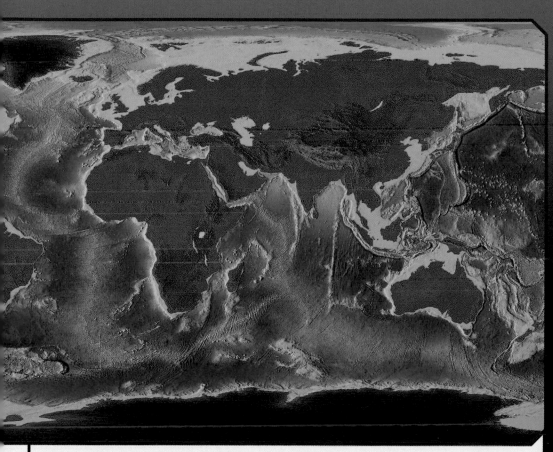

This map illustrates global land and undersea elevation, with the deepest areas of the ocean in dark blue.

Agreements adopted by UNCLOS in 1994 allow coastal countries to claim exclusive rights to resources located within the continental shelf bordering a country's coastline. In the early 21st century, several countries with Arctic coastlines made competing claims on the extended continental shelf regions within the Arctic Ocean.

Glomar Challenger, a positioned drill ship (a vessel equipped with a drilling derrick, moon pool, and special positioning equipment) to remove material from the ocean floor to depths of more than 20,000 feet (6,000 meters). The samples obtained through this effort helped scientists learn about the origin and history of Earth.

The project's successors, the Ocean Drilling Program and, starting in 2003, the Integrated Ocean Drilling Program, further advanced scientific exploration of the world's oceans. The Ocean Drilling Program was an international partnership of scientists and research institutions. From 1985 to 2003, more than 2,500 international scientists sailed on more than 100 expeditions aboard the *JOIDES Resolution* to explore Earth's history and structure as recorded in the ocean basins. Featuring a six-story laboratory area and a derrick 200 feet (60 meters) tall, the *JOIDES Resolution* can drill in water up to 30,000 feet (9,140 meters) deep. The *JOIDES Resolution* continues to serve science today as part of the International Ocean Discovery Program, an international research effort that coordinates expeditions to study sediments and rocks beneath the ocean floor.

RESEARCH VESSELS TODAY

Vessels are one of the most critical elements of any ocean expedition. The types of vessels used today for exploration, mining, and undersea construction projects are varied and include surface vessels, moored platforms, drillships, floating instrument platforms, submersibles, and semisubmersibles.

The advantage of surface vessels and plat-forms is their size and stability. Vessels such as the *Okeanos Explorer* are amply equipped for ocean exploration. Operated by the National Oceanic and Atmospheric Administration, the *Okeanos Explorer* is a 224-foot (68-meter) sur-face vessel featuring a satellite dome mounted high above its bridge. The ship is used for a variety of expeditions, such as exploring and mapping marine habitats.

Submersibles are underwater vehicles that allow direct and detailed observation at vari-ous depths and are widely used for undersea exploration. The first deep-sea submersible capable of carrying passengers was *Alvin*, a three-person submarine operated by Woods Hole Oceanographic Institution. Since its first

The *Remora 2000* is a two-seater research submarine used for archaeological research.

launch in 1964, *Alvin* has embarked on more than 4,600 dives, carrying roughly 13,000 scientists and other researchers on expeditions of the oceans' depths.

Modern technology has given rise to customized research vessels, satellite and electronic navigation, and sophisticated sonar systems for use in mapping the ocean basins. Since the late 20th century, deep-sea robots have been used to collect samples from ocean floors, inspect oil rigs, and do underwater photography. These robots are less expensive to

operate than manned submersibles, and they have similar abilities.

REMOTE SENSING OF THE OCEANS

One of the fundamental problems faced by oceanographers is the sheer size of the oceans and the consequent need to rely on special surface vessels and submersibles for direct measurements. It can be very costly to operate either type of vessel on long deep-sea expeditions. Moreover, observations from such craft can provide only a partial picture of oceanic phenomena and processes in terms of both space and time. Consequently, there has been considerable interest in taking advantage of remote-sensing techniques in oceanography, particularly those that use satellites. Remote sensing allows measurements to be made of vast areas of ocean repeated at intervals in time.

The first satellite devoted to oceanographic observations was Seasat, which orbited Earth for three months in 1978. Its polar orbit made it possible to provide coverage of 95 percent of the major oceans every 36 hours. Seasat carried radiometers for observations at visible, infrared, and microwave wavelengths, along

with radar scatterometers, imaging radar, and an altimeter. This array of instruments yielded much data, including an estimation of sea-surface temperatures, net radiation inputs to the sea surface, wave heights, and wind speeds close to the sea surface. In addition, patterns of near-surface sediment movement and other information were derived from an analysis of the satellite images.

CHAPTER 2

PHYSICAL AND CHEMICAL OCEANOGRAPHY

Physical and chemical oceanography are studies of the physical and chemical properties of Earth and its oceans. Physical oceanographers study water properties such as temperature and salinity and the oceanic transmission of electrical, optical, and acoustical energy. They may also be concerned with the exchange of thermal, or heat, energy at the air-sea surface and the general motion of seawater. Chemical oceanographers identify the dissolved elements in seawater and the ocean's numerous chemical and biochemical cycles. They also devise geochemical models to explain the origin and development of the oceans.

CHEMICAL COMPONENTS OF SEAWATER

Billions of years ago, Earth was enveloped in clouds so thick that sunlight could not

penetrate them and was so hot that no moisture could fall to its surface. As the planet cooled, rain began to fall continuously for centuries, pouring into the deep ocean basin and carrying with it the minerals of the continents, including the salts. Today the salt in the oceans would cover the continents with a 490-foot-thick (150-meter-thick) layer.

The solid material carried to the oceans by rivers is deposited mainly near the shore, often forming such great river deltas as that of the Mississippi. Dissolved materials gradually mix throughout the oceans and become part of the great salt content of the seas.

There is much more salt in seawater than in river water. Comparing the percentages of the various salts present shows a significant difference in composition between the two kinds of water. The rivers of today are probably similar to those that existed in the past. The differences in the composition of river water and seawater are due largely to chemical reactions that take place in the oceans. Most of these reactions remove material from seawater. Living organisms, for example, consume some of the elements as food, then die and sink to the ocean floor. This dead organic material is chemically "sticky" and may draw rare elements from the water.

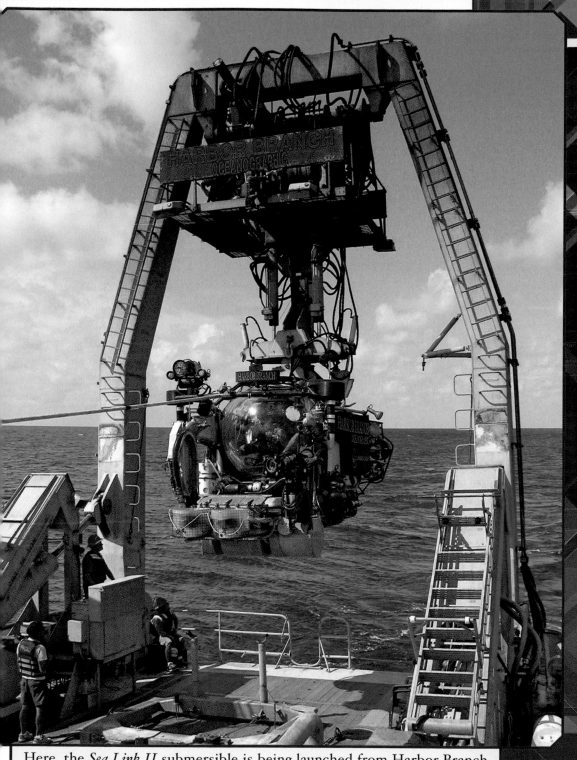

Here, the *Sea Link II* submersible is being launched from Harbor Branch Oceanographic Institution in Fort Pierce, Florida. Retired from service in 2011, the vessel could accommodate four people.

The mineral particles suspended in river water settle at the mouths of the rivers or are carried out to sea, where they settle to the ocean floor. They, like the organic material, remove elements from the seawater solution as they settle.

Materials dissolved in ocean water may also be removed by chemical reactions with substances in the seafloor itself. These reactions, in turn, form new minerals. Also, some of the dissolved salts are blown out of the water by the wind, along with the ocean spray. Most of the chloride in river water is in the process of being returned to the ocean after a wind-borne escape.

TYPES OF ELEMENTS IN SEAWATER

The chemical elements that are easily removed from seawater by the processes mentioned, leaving only small amounts in solution, are called trace elements. It is probable that every element that exists in the Earth is also present in ocean water, though many elements are too scarce to be measured.

The most abundant elements in the oceans are hydrogen and oxygen. Together they make up water, and they also exist separately in

the sea as dissolved gases. Also abundant are sodium, magnesium, calcium, and potassium, as well as sulfates and chlorides. These substances become well mixed into the oceans and are always found in the same proportions. They consistently make up fixed percentages of the dissolved materials in any sample of seawater. The rare elements, especially those that are nutrients for plants and other living things, are found in varying amounts.

THE FORMATION OF SEAWATER

The chemical processes involved in the formation of seawater can be described in terms of Earth's geochemical balance. Originally, the Earth's crust was composed of igneous rock, the composition of which is known. Over long periods of time, the oceans and the great layers of sedimentary rock were formed. By considering the differences in composition between igneous and sedimentary rocks and then estimating the amount of rock that has been changed from igneous to sedimentary, it is possible to calculate the total amounts of the various elements which have been delivered to the oceans.

The elements sodium, magnesium, calcium, and potassium are metals and commonly form

cations (or positively charged ions) in solution. A significant fraction of these four elements is left in seawater, but some other metals, such as iron and aluminum, have been almost entirely removed.

The elements chlorine, bromine, sulfur, and boron are also present in the ocean, in quantities much too abundant to have been derived from the weathering of rocks. These elements are nonmetals and tend to form anions (negatively charged ions) in solution. They are found in volcanic gases, and it seems certain that they were delivered to the oceans through billions of years of volcanic eruptions. It is not possible to estimate what fraction of these anions has been removed from the seas.

SALINITY AND DENSITY OF SEAWATER

The salinity of ocean water is given as a percentage. It is defined as the ratio of the weight of salt in a given volume of water to the weight of the water. The usual notation is in parts per thousand indicated by the symbol o/oo. Thus, ocean water with a salinity of 35 o/oo has 3.5 pounds (1.6 kilograms) of salt in each 100 pounds (45.4 kilograms) of seawater. The salinity depends upon the balance maintained

between the evaporation of water from the surface of the sea and the amount of freshwater that is being returned to the sea by rivers and rain.

When seawater evaporates, the salt is left to form a more concentrated solution. In the central region of the oceans, therefore, if more water is lost by evaporation than is returned by rainfall, the surface salinity will be greater than it is in areas where rainfall is adequate to replace the water lost by evaporation. In coastal waters, the salinity at the surface is usually less than it is in the central ocean basins because the flow of fresh river water from the land dilutes the seawater.

The density of seawater is determined by its temperature and salinity. Water becomes denser as it gets colder or saltier. The heaviest water, therefore, has both very low temperature and very high salinity.

How the Ocean Is Heated

The Sun's light penetrates many feet into seawater, and far from land the ocean is deep blue and as transparent as pure distilled water. Along the coasts, however, its transparency is reduced by the growth of tiny plants and

organisms called plankton. The latter are living things of the sea that cannot swim against the current but rather drift along on currents. Plantlike plankton are called phytoplankton; animal-like plankton are called zooplankton. Most planktonic organisms are microscopic. Organic-decay products from dead organisms are also present in coastal waters. Collectively the organic matter from plankton and their decaying remains gives coastal water its characteristic green color. The transparency of coastal seawater is also reduced by the sediment carried into it by rivers.

As ocean water absorbs the Sun's radiation, the surface layer becomes heated. This heat can be lost in several ways, the two most important being evaporation and radiation. An average of about 36 inches (91 centimeters) of water evaporates from the surface of the oceans each year. This amount is approximately equal to some 88,000 cubic miles (1,316,000 cubic kilometers). In some regions—such as off the coast of Labrador, where cold, dry air flows over the warmer air of the Gulf Stream—the evaporation rate in winter may be half an inch per day. The evaporation of one cubic inch (16 cubic centimeters) of water requires the same amount of heat that would have to be removed from 1,000 cubic inches (16,000 cubic centimeters) of water to cool it one degree Fahrenheit.

The temperatures of the oceans may vary by time of day and season. On a clear day in March, for example, the ocean surface becomes heated; after the Sun sets, the same amount of heat may be lost. During spring and summer, more heat is absorbed than is lost, and the temperature of the ocean's surface layer increases. The wind and waves mix the heat downward, causing a sharp thermocline, or temperature gradient. In autumn, more heat is lost to the atmosphere than is gained by the ocean.

It takes more heat to raise the temperature of a given volume of water one degree Fahrenheit than it does to raise the temperature of the same volume of sand one degree. This, together with the fact that the warmed water is mixed many tens of feet deep, makes the oceans huge reservoirs of heat. Heat is stored in summer and slowly given up in winter.

The surface of the sea is usually warmer than the adjacent land in winter and cooler than the land in summer. The oceans therefore have a moderating effect upon the climates of coastal cities. Cities farther inland generally experience greater season-to-season variations in climate.

During the summer months, the mixing of seawater may carry the heat of the Sun's

radiation to a depth of several hundred feet. However, this is only a small part of the total ocean depth. Below this layer of seasonal change the oceans are cold and dark. Since cold water is heavier than warm water, the world's oceans below a few thousand feet contain water that originally sank either close to the Antarctic continent or far to the north in the Atlantic Ocean off Greenland.

Occasionally, water becomes very heavy because of its high salinity. An example of this is the Mediterranean Sea. The water flowing outward through the Strait of Gibraltar has greater salinity than the adjacent water of the Atlantic Ocean, and because it is heavier, it sinks. This Mediterranean flow can be tracked as a tongue of high-salinity water most of the way across the Atlantic Ocean.

Water having a characteristic temperature and salinity is called a water mass. The measurement of temperature and salinity is one method oceanographers use to trace the movement of water masses. For example, in the Atlantic Ocean the cold, low-salinity Antarctic Bottom Water can be tracked as it moves northward along the seafloor. However, it is easier to track the low-salinity tongue of Antarctic Intermediate Water, which moves northward at a depth of about 3,000 feet (900 meters). Between these two water masses, most of the depth is filled by Atlantic Deep Water, which takes on its characteristic temperature and salinity in the north and moves southward, mixing slowly with the surrounding water.

MIXING OF THE OCEANS

The exact manner in which deep water masses move is still unknown to oceanographers, as are their speeds of movement. Their movement is slow, but probably not steady. It is possible that water masses move in whirls and eddies very much as smoke rises from a slowly burning fire.

The oceans of the world are interconnected and flow through the great Southern (Antarctic) Ocean surrounding Antarctica. By way of this ocean, the water from the Atlantic Ocean can flow into the Indian and Pacific Oceans.

Consider a hypothetical experiment. If a cubic mile (4.2 cubic kilometers) of seawater halfway between the surface and the seafloor in the middle of the Atlantic Ocean were dyed red, the movement of the individual molecules of water could be traced. The cube would probably drift slowly southward at a speed

THE SOUND CHANNEL IN THE SEA

Sound waves travel better through water than do light and radio waves. This fact is employed by ships at sea to locate the position of submarines or schools of fish. The technique of using high-frequency sound waves with sonar devices is called echo ranging. The method is similar to the way in which the position of an airplane or a ship is found by echo ranging using radio waves with radar devices.

Sound can travel much farther in the ocean than in the air. One reason for this is the sound channel that exists in the deep ocean. The velocity of sound increases with increasing temperature and pressure. There is a depth in the ocean at which the velocity of sound is at a minimum. Sound energy becomes trapped in this low-velocity sound channel.

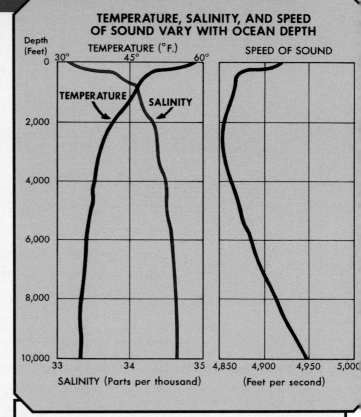

TEMPERATURE, SALINITY, AND SPEED OF SOUND VARY WITH OCEAN DEPTH

SALINITY (Parts per thousand)

(Feet per second)

The graph on the left shows how temperature and salinity vary with depth. The graph on the right shows how the speed of sound varies with depth in the ocean.

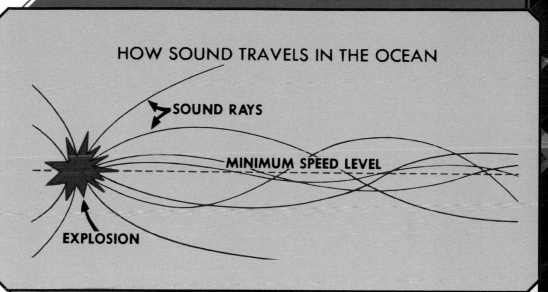

HOW SOUND TRAVELS IN THE OCEAN

SOUND RAYS

MINIMUM SPEED LEVEL

EXPLOSION

Sound rays transmitted in nearly horizontal directions in the ocean are refracted toward the minimum speed level.

The sound channel extends continuously through most areas of the world's oceans. For example, if a small explosive charge is detonated in the sound channel near San Francisco, California, the sound can be detected by a hydrophone suspended in the sound channel near the Hawaiian Islands, some 2,500 miles (4,000 kilometers) away.

of about 50 miles (80 kilometers) a year. But it would mix with the surrounding water at a much faster rate. Because the density of seawater increases with depth, the water mixes horizontally more easily than vertically.

In time, the red cube would become a pink disk with a vertical dimension of perhaps two miles (three kilometers) and a horizontal diameter of about one thousand miles (1,600 kilometers). Pink water that reached the surface would mix with the surrounding water faster than would the water that was two miles deep. The dyed water would eventually find its way to the Southern Ocean and then to the Pacific Ocean and the Indian Ocean. Finally, all ocean waters would become pale pink as the dyed molecules found their way into oceans at all depths. How long would this take? Some oceanographers believe the mixing process would require at least a thousand years.

CHAPTER 3

BIOLOGICAL OCEANOGRAPHY

B iological oceanography is the study of the populations of plants, animals, and other organisms of the sea. It deals especially with the distribution of these living communities, their numerical growth, how one population affects another, and how they are influenced by the environment in which they live. For instance, the number of fish caught by commercial fishing fleets in a certain area of the continental shelf may depend upon the amount of fish food present in a particular year. What is this fish food? Some kinds of fish feed on zooplankton, which tend to inhabit the upper waters. The zooplankton may be more numerous in some years than in others. This may be due to variations in the abundance of phytoplankton (on which zooplankton themselves feed), variations in currents, or variations in the temperature of the water. Other kinds of fish eat animals that live on the bottom of the ocean. When conditions favor the growth of

These colorful underwater flora are an example of the biological diversity that exists below the ocean's surface.

these bottom-dwelling animals, the fishes also increase in number.

THREE GROUPS OF SEA LIFE

Scientists divide the life of the sea into three groups. One group consists of the animals that are able to swim strongly enough to move against a current. This group, called the nekton, is made up for the most part of fishes but also includes squid and whales.

Another group, the benthos, is composed of all the animals, plants, and other organisms that live on or in the sea bottom. This group includes seaweeds, crabs, worms, and similar marine life.

A third group—which is the least noticeable and was the last to be discovered—is the most important of all. This group is the plankton, which consists of thousands of kinds of mostly tiny living things. They do not, as is often supposed, lie on the ocean surface. Instead, they are suspended in the water at various depths. Planktonic organisms are therefore carried throughout the oceans by the currents.

The portion of plankton consisting of plants and plantlike organisms, such as algae and some bacteria, is called phytoplankton.

Zooplankton are animal-like forms of plankton.

Many of these organisms are single celled and so small that they cannot be seen without a microscope. Most of the zooplankton group, which comprises animals and animal-like organisms, are only a fraction of an inch in size, though some—such as the larger jellyfishes—are a foot or more in diameter.

Plankton is very important because only plants, algae, and some bacteria can use sunlight to manufacture the carbohydrates that all animals need in their food. This process is called photosynthesis. In order to obtain carbohydrates, animals must eat either photosynthetic organisms or other animals that have eaten photosynthetic organisms. However, sunlight penetrates only a short distance into the sea, and most ocean water is in absolute darkness. There is not enough light there for photosynthesis to occur. Without phytoplankton, most of the ocean would be a vast liquid desert, unable to support any life. The phytoplankton that float in the well-lighted upper layers of the ocean perform photosynthesis, thereby making the nutrients needed for nearly all other life-forms in the sea. During spring and summer the surface waters of the oceans have an abundance of blooms of these mostly minute organisms.

The growth of phytoplankton frequently removes all nutrient elements—principally nitrogen, phosphorus, and silicon—from the surface waters. In spring and summer, the surface waters are warm and light and do not easily mix with the cold, heavy deep water. As a result, new nutrients are not available in the surface waters.

Eventually the blooms fail for lack of food, and the organisms die and sink into the depths.

As they descend, their remains are broken down by bacteria. The nutrient elements within the remains are then liberated and return to the seawater solution in the depths. Upwelling is a process of vertical water motion whereby subsurface water and its suspended nutrients are carried toward the surface. The most pronounced coastal upwellings are found off the western United States, Peru, Morocco, South Africa, western Africa, western Australia, and south of the Aleutian chain. The reverse process, downwelling, completes the cyclical movement of bodies of water.

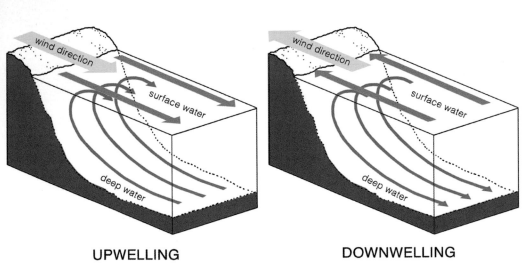

UPWELLING

DOWNWELLING

Upwelling typically results when offshore winds blow surface waters out to sea and deeper waters rise to replace them. Downwelling occurs when onshore winds cause surface waters to pile up and sink.

Downwelling and upwelling do not necessarily occur in the same areas. As a result of upwelling, extensive fishing and kelp areas are found off the continents of Africa and North and South America, large bird populations produce economic guano deposits in Peru, and near the Antarctic Convergence in the Atlantic there is an unusually large standing crop of plankton that supports krill, the main food of whales. Such coastal areas are also provided with nutrient-rich waters for mariculture, or the farming of organisms in the sea.

PHYTOPLANKTON

The main components of phytoplankton (which is Greek for "plant wanderers") are plantlike organisms that include diatoms, dinoflagellates, coccolithophorids, green algae, and cyanobacteria (formerly known as blue-green algae). Many of them are microscopic and single celled. The growth of these organisms, which photosynthesize, depends on a delicate balance between nutrient enrichment by vertical mixing, often limited by the availability of nitrogen, and the availability of light. Diatoms are one-celled or colonial protists with patterned glass coverings. Each glass, or silicon dioxide, box is ornamented with

THE WATER CYCLE

Water must be readily available to support life and its activities. It may seem that water is always available since Earth is literally surrounded by it: up to 4 percent of the atmosphere near ground level may consist of water vapor. Also, many thousands of lakes, rivers, and streams are scattered over Earth's surface. The vast oceans, almost an unending source of water, cover more than 129 million square miles (335 million square kilometers) and contain almost 330,000,000 cubic miles (1,386,000,000 cubic kilometers) of water. Yet, with all this water, there are parts of Earth that are arid. The manner in which water circulates between Earth and the atmosphere determines where ample water supplies can be found and used.

If no forces except gravity were at work, the world's water would settle into the ocean basins and remain there. The land surfaces would become lifeless deserts. Water, however, does not stagnate in the oceans. It is continually evaporating from the oceans and other bodies of water by the heat of the Sun and blown by the winds across sea and land. Thus an immense amount of water is always suspended in the atmosphere in the form of vapor. When certain weather conditions prevail in the atmosphere, some of the water vapor condenses into droplets of liquid water, ice crystals, or both—forming clouds. When such clouds accumulate more moisture than they can hold, the water is returned to the land as rain or snow. This process of moving water out of the oceans, into the atmosphere, and back to the land and oceans is called the water cycle.

species-specific designs, making them popular with microscopists.

Some of the thousands of kinds of phytoplankton swim feebly by lashing a whiplike thread appendage called a flagellum. These dinoflagellates are known for their bioluminescence, or phosphorescence, a "cold light" similar to that of fireflies. Since they emit a toxin, dinoflagellates can be extremely poisonous when present in great numbers. In plumes they are known to color the water red, brown, or even black. Red tides in the Gulf of Mexico and in Walvis Bay, Namibia, are often accompanied by mass mortality of fish, crabs, and other animals that wash up on the beach. A strong toxin of red tides, when accumulated in mussels and clams and consumed by humans, can lead to illness or death.

ZOOPLANKTON

Zooplankton are animal-like forms of plankton. Among these are the larval and adult forms of some animal species and certain protozoans. During the temporary larval stages, some benthic and nektonic animals appear quite different from the adults into which they mature. These immature animals are able to populate new areas by drifting with the currents.

Copepods are zooplankton of great ecological importance, providing food for many species of fish. Most of the 13,000 known copepod species are free-living marine forms, occurring throughout the world's oceans.

Copepods are small crustaceans that are holoplankton, or organisms that are plankton throughout their life cycles. There are probably more copepods in the world than there are all other animals combined (though the animal-like protozoans are even more numerous). The primary herbivorous animals of the sea, copepods are vital to marine ecosystems.

They graze off the aquatic pastures of phytoplankton and provide a link between the primary production of algae, plants, and cyanobacteria and the numerous large and small carnivores. Most copepods are tiny but some can be as big as a grain of rice.

Other abundant holoplankton are the single-celled foraminiferans and radiolarians. The foraminiferans have skeletons made of calcium carbonate, and radiolarians have skeletons made of silicon dioxide. Jellyfishes are among the largest planktonic organisms. Transparent arrowworms, or glass worms, are bottom dwellers with large jaws designed to seize copepods and other small animals.

Fish and Marine Mammals

The majority of ocean fish are coastal, or littoral; very few are diadromous, living part of their lives in freshwater and part in the oceans. The familiar fish species caught for human consumption make up only a fraction of the world fish population. The most abundant fishes of the ocean—cyclostomes—are not commercially sought and live 1,000 to 3,000 feet (300 to 900 meters) below the surface. These small, transparent, and luminescent species

are so abundant that, as a deep scattering layer, they reflect the sound waves of echo-ranging instruments.

The marine mammals, also part of the nekton, include the seals, sea lions, sea otters, manatees, porpoises, and whales. Some whales consume zooplankton by straining them from the water through horny plates (baleen or whalebone). The killer whale preys upon fishes, penguins, porpoises, seals, and sea lions.

CHAPTER 4

GEOLOGICAL OCEANOGRAPHY

Geological oceanography is one of the broadest fields in the Earth sciences. Researchers in this branch of oceanography are involved in the study of the topography, structure, and geological processes of the ocean floor.

THE CONTINENTS AND OCEAN BASINS

The largest features of Earth's surface are the continents and ocean basins. The four major ocean basins (Arctic, Atlantic, Indian, and Pacific) are bound by landmasses and major oceanic ridges. Each continent is rimmed by a submerged, gently sloping continental margin. This includes the relatively flat continental shelf, generally found at depths of less than 600 feet (180 meters) with a width of a few miles to more than 200 miles (320 kilometers). At the shelf break portion of the margin, there is a rise in the continental shelf before the continental

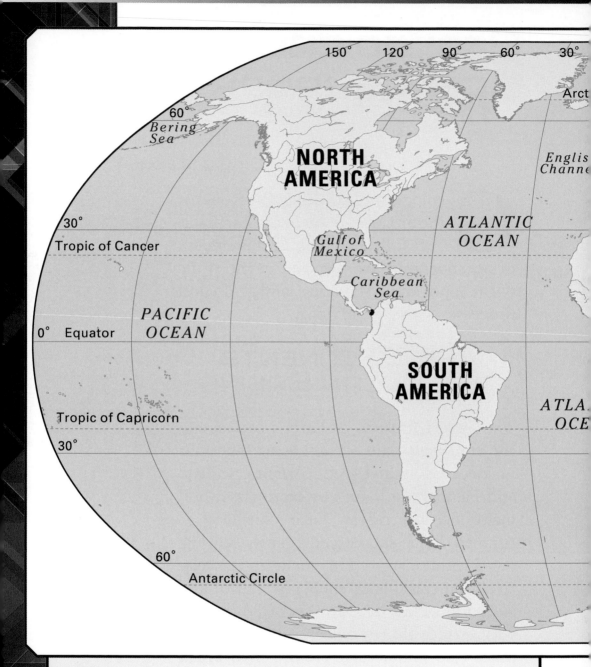

Earth's oceans cover nearly 71 percent of the planet's surface.

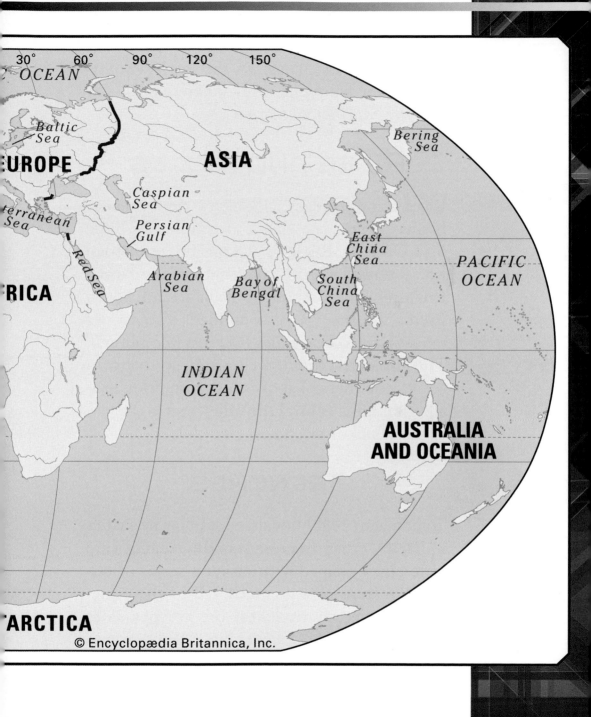

© Encyclopædia Britannica, Inc.

slope begins its plunge to the deep-sea bottom. Deep submarine canyons frequently cut into the continental margin.

RISES AND RIDGES

Rises and ridges, flanked by smaller basins, divide the major ocean basins. The Mid-Oceanic Ridge is a continuous medial rift system that spans the length of the North Atlantic, South Atlantic, Indian, and South Pacific oceans for a combined distance of more than 40,000 miles (64,000 kilometers). This broad fractured swell, rising up to 9,000 feet (2,700 meters) above the ocean floor, usually contains a central rift valley that is the site of earthquake epicenters.

TRENCHES

Trenches are highly localized submarine gashes in Earth's crust. In cross section, trenches are generally V-shaped with either a series of terracelike steps or a dramatic fall to the ocean floor. In deeper trenches, the steeper sides are toward land. Trenches lie mainly around the Pacific but also occur in the northern borders of the Indian Ocean, in the outer loops of the Caribbean, and in the Scotia Arc, an island system in the South Atlantic. They mark some of the deepest spots in the ocean: the Mariana Trench off the coast of Guam, the Tonga Trench in the South Pacific, and the Philippine Trench. Troughs are elongated depressions with contours more gradual than those of trenches. Some trenches are partially filled with sediments and appear as troughs.

Seamounts

Isolated elevations that rise at least 3,000 feet (900 meters) above the surrounding deep-sea floor are called seamounts. Although more than 1,400 have been listed for the Pacific Basin alone, some 90 percent are thought to remain undiscovered. Usually basaltic volcanoes, these undersea mountains often occur as long chains, as they do in the Hawaiian Islands. A seapeak is a seamount with a pointed summit. Guyots are flat-topped seamounts that became smooth-planed by the action of wind and water when the submarine volcanoes were at sea level.

Abyssal Hills

Abyssal plains are flat areas of the seafloor about 10,000 to 20,000 feet (3,000 to 6,000

RECENT GEOLOGICAL HISTORY

The continents and their accompanying fragments of oceanic crust ride piggyback over the lithosphere. In the 1970s and '80s the proof of continental formation, fragmentation, and drift was uncovered. Erupting from the mid-oceanic ridges, basalts record the alternating polarity of Earth's magnetic field. The magnetic field has reversed itself in 500,000- to 2,000,000-year intervals during recent geologic time. Marine geologists are able to determine the rate of the seafloor spreading by measuring the magnetic stripe patterns in the floor. The Atlantic seafloor spreads 1 to 4 inches (2.5 to 10 centimeters) every year. Special contour maps, in which the seafloor is divided into age zones, show that the ocean basins are about 200 million years old.

Ten thousand years ago the sea level was about 200 feet (60 meters) lower than it is today. The rise in sea level since the last major glacial advances in the Pleistocene era has contributed to the erosion of coastlines. Continuation and, in some areas, acceleration of present rates of sea-level rise continue to have profound effects on humans, particularly those living on the margins of the sea. Among the causes is the melting of glaciers as a result of global warming.

meters) below the water's surface, generally adjacent to the continents. Rising from these plains are abyssal hills less than 3,000 feet (900 meters) high and about 10 times as wide. They are variously formed by volcanism, folding and

faulting, and sediment draping over older buried seamounts or hills. The abyssal zone is the world's largest ecological unit, occupying more than three-quarters of the total area of the oceans and more than half of the area of the globe.

OCEANIC CRUST

Oceanic crust is typically composed of three layers that overlie the mantle. Unconsolidated sediments, averaging about a third of a mile (a half kilometer) in thickness, make up the top layer. Next is the consolidated volcanic layer, about a mile (1.6 kilometers) thick. It is thinner in shallow water and thicker in the Pacific than in the Atlantic Ocean. On the bottom is the basaltic or oceanic layer, about 3 miles (5 kilometers) in thickness. It is principally composed of rocks rich in magnesium and iron, especially basalt. Surface hills are common in the oceanic layer. In some places the oceanic layer is not covered by the other two layers.

Studies of the magnetic properties of minerals in the oceanic crust provide information about the structure and movements of the crust. Magnetic patterns on both sides of oceanic rift valleys show that new seafloor is produced at these rifts and moves horizontally

away from the spreading centers. Over the past 200 million years, this process has produced all of the crust of the present seafloor.

SUBMARINE GEOLOGICAL PROCESSES

The geological processes of the deep sea are relatively slow compared to those on land. A striking difference between land and sea is the lack of significant erosion in the deep sea. Sedimentary deposits accumulate in the deep sea at a rate of only a fraction of an inch every thousand years. Once deposited, marine sediments are unlikely to be eroded and redeposited because bottom currents are generally weak. Deep-sea pelagic sediments thus offer the most complete historical records of organic evolution, temperature changes during ice ages, and other geological patterns.

CLASTIC SEDIMENTATION

Most clastic sediment—rock and soil eroded from the land—is first deposited on the continental shelf, mainly in tidal environments, in deltas, and along beaches. The rest of the sediment continues out to sea. Winds and currents carry fine-grained particles offshore where they ultimately settle to the ocean floor. Along the continental margins, sediment is carried by turbidity currents that flow downhill because they are denser than the surrounding water. These underwater avalanches help explain the formation of submarine canyons, continental rises, and the flat abyssal plains of the deep-sea floor. Deposits of the rise and abyssal plain consisting of graded beds of sand, silt, and clay that have formed in this way are called turbidites.

CHEMICAL AND BIOLOGICAL DEPOSITION

Most of the near-shore and shallow-water sediments are calcareous—consisting of calcium carbonate derived from the shells or hard coverings of dead marine animals. Some of the larger contributors include clams, mussels, oysters, scallops, snails, and slugs; smaller sources are the microscopic organisms of the sea, including those that make up coral and algal reefs.

Deep-sea deposits are located in less than 13,000 feet (4,000 meters) of water, where much of the ocean floor is covered with an ooze (deposits of soft mud) made of the shells

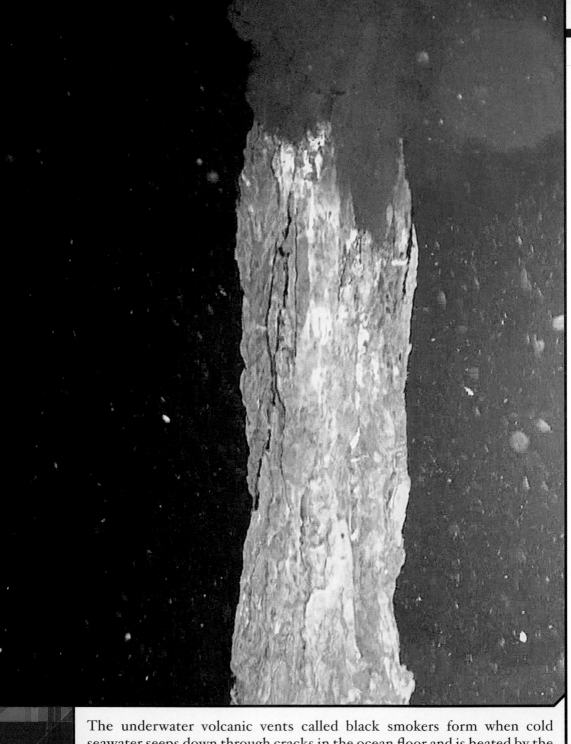

The underwater volcanic vents called black smokers form when cold seawater seeps down through cracks in the ocean floor and is heated by the hot magma (molten rock) below. The heated water, now rich with dissolved minerals from the ocean crust, gushes up through the vent.

of foraminiferans. Below this depth there is less calcium carbonate, and the falling shelled organisms begin to dissolve while settling or soon after coming to rest on the bottom. The depth of water below which calcium carbonate begins to dissolve is called the calcium carbonate compensation depth. Calcium carbonates are the most abundant biological sediments on the seafloor; oozes of silica, however, form below the compensation depth. Diatom oozes, consisting of the remains of green unicellular algae, are found mostly in the Pacific and Antarctic oceans.

VOLCANISM

Submarine volcanoes produce lava flows, volcanic ash, and fine-grained lava sediment on the seafloor. Ocean-ridge volcanism produces basaltic seafloor crust that sometimes builds plateaus, such as Iceland, that rise above sea level. Subsea earthquakes are associated with mid-oceanic ridge systems and subduction zones where plate boundaries converge.

CHAPTER 5

STUDY OF WATERS CLOSE TO EARTH'S SURFACE

Hydrology is mainly concerned with waters close to the land surface of Earth. It deals with that part of the water cycle from the arrival of water at the land surface as precipitation to its eventual loss from the land either by evaporation or transpiration back to the atmosphere or by surface and subsurface flow to the sea.

The field of hydrology includes a number of more specialized subdisciplines. For example, the field of hydraulics is concerned with the mechanics and dynamics of water in its liquid state. Hydrography is the description and mapping of the bodies of water of Earth's surface (including the oceans), with a particular concern for navigation charts. Hydrometry involves measurements of surface water, particularly precipitation and streamflow. Hydrometeorology focuses on water in the lower boundary layer of the atmosphere. Groundwater hydrology, hydrogeology, and soil water physics are

Hydrology focuses on the study of waters close to the land surface, such as in rivers and streams.

concerned with different aspects of subsurface water. Engineering hydrology is concerned with the design of man-made structures that control the flow and use of water.

Underlying all the hydrologic sciences is the concept of water balance. This is an expression of the water cycle for an area of the land surface in terms of conservation of mass. In a simple form the water balance may be expressed as

$$S = P - Q - E - G,$$

where S is the change of water storage in the area over a given time period, P is the precipitation input during that time period, Q is the stream discharge from the area, E is the total of evaporation and transpiration to the atmosphere from the area, and G is the subsurface outflow. Most hydrologic studies are concerned with evaluating one or more terms of the water balance equation. Because of the difficulties in quantifying the movement of water across the boundaries of an area under study, the water balance equation is most easily applied to an area draining to a particular measurement point on a stream channel. This area is called a catchment (or sometimes a watershed in the United States). The line separating adjacent catchments is known as a topographical divide, or simply a divide. The following sections describe the study of the different elements of the catchment water balance and the way in which they affect the response of catchments over time under different climatic regimes.

PRECIPITATION

Precipitation results from the condensation of water from the atmosphere as air is cooled to the dew point, the temperature at which the air becomes saturated with respect to water vapor. The cooling process is usually initiated by uplift of the air, which may result from a number of causes, including convection, orographic effects over mountain ranges, or frontal effects at the boundaries of air masses of different characteristics. Condensation within the atmosphere requires the presence of condensation nuclei to initiate droplet formation. Some of the condensate may be carried considerable distances as clouds before being released as rain or snow, depending on the local temperatures. Some precipitation in the form of dew or fog results from condensation at or near the land surface. In some areas, such as the coastal Northwest of the United States, dew and fog drip can contribute significantly to the water balance. The formation of hail requires a sequence of condensation and freezing episodes, resulting from successive periods of uplift. Hailstones usually show a pattern of concentric rings of ice as a result.

Direct measurements of precipitation are made by a variety of gauges, all of which consist of some form of funnel that directs the infalling water to some storage container. Storage gauges simply store the incident precipitation, and the accumulated water is usually measured on a daily, weekly, or monthly basis.

Recording gauges allow rates of precipitation to be determined.

Rainfall volumes are usually converted to units of depth—volume per unit area. Measurements obtained from different types of rain gauges are not directly comparable because of varying exposure, wind, and splash effects. The most accurate type of gauge is the ground-level gauge, in which the opening of the gauge is placed level with the ground surface and surrounded by an antisplash grid. Rain gauge catches decrease as the opening is raised above the ground, particularly in areas subject to high winds. In areas of significant snowfall, however, it may be necessary to raise the rain gauge so that its opening is clear of the snow surface. Various shields for the gauge opening have been tried in an effort to offset wind effects. Wind effects are greater for snow than for rain and for small drops or light rainfall than for large drops.

An impression of the spatial distribution of precipitation intensity can be achieved through indirect measurements of precipitation, in particular radar scattering. The relationship between rainfall intensity and measured radar signals depends on various factors, including the type of precipitation and the distribution of drop size. Radar measurements are often

Rainfall refers not just to rain but to all precipitation—all the water that falls on an area, including rain, snow, sleet, hail, dew, and frost.

used in conjunction with rain gauges to allow on-line calibration in converting the radar signal to precipitation amounts. The radar measurements are, however, at a much larger spatial scale. Resolution of 5 to 10 square kilometers is common for operational systems. Even so, this provides a much better picture of the spatial patterns of precipitation over large catchment areas than has been previously possible. The use of satellite remote sensing to determine rainfall volumes is still in its early stages, but the technique appears

likely to prove useful for estimating amounts of precipitation in remote areas.

The measurement of inputs of snow to the catchment water balance is also a difficult problem. The most basic technique involves the snow course, a series of stakes to measure snow depths. Snowfalls can, however, vary greatly in density, depending primarily on the temperature history of snow formation. Accumulated snow changes its density over time prior to melting. Snow density can be measured by weighing a sample of known volume taken in a standard metal cylinder. Other techniques for measuring snowfall include the use of snow pillows, which record the changing weight of snow lying above them, or the use of rain gauges fitted with heating elements, which melt the snow as it falls. These techniques are subject to wind effects, both during a storm and between storms because of redistribution of snow by the wind.

Summary statistics on precipitation are usually produced on the basis of daily, monthly, and annual amounts falling at a given location or over a catchment area. The frequency at which a rainfall of a certain volume occurs within a certain period is also important to hydrologic analysis. The assessment of this frequency, or the recurrence interval of the rainfall from the sample of available data, is a statistical problem generally involving the assumption of a particular probability distribution to represent the characteristics of rainfalls. Such analyses must assume that this distribution is not changing over time, even though it has been shown that in some areas of the world climatic change may cause rainfall statistics to vary.

It has long been speculated that rainfalls may exhibit cyclic patterns over long periods of time, and considerable effort has been expended in searching for such cycles. In some areas the annual seasonal cycle is of paramount importance, but demonstrations of longer periods have not proved to be applicable in a general way.

Patterns of rainfall intensity and duration are of great importance to the hydrologist in predicting catchment discharges and water availability and in dealing with floods, droughts, land drainage, and soil erosion. Rainfalls vary both within and between rainstorms, sometimes dramatically, depending on the type and scale of the storm and its velocity of movement. Within a storm, the average intensity tends to decrease with an increase in the storm area.

On a larger scale, seasonal variations in rainfall vary with climate. Humid temperate areas

tend to have rainfalls that are fairly evenly distributed throughout the year; Mediterranean areas have a winter peak with low summer rainfalls; savanna areas have a double peak in rainfall; and equatorial areas again have a relatively even distribution of rainfall over the course of the year. Average annual rainfalls also vary considerably. The minimum recorded long-term average is 0.03 inch (0.76 millimeter) at Arica, Chile; the maximum 468.4 inches (11,897 millimeters) at Tutunendo, Colombia. The maximum recorded rainfall intensities are 1.5 inches (38 millimeters) in one minute (Barot, Guadeloupe, 1970); 73.6 inches (1,870 millimeters) in a single day (Cilaos, Réunion, 1952); and 1,041.8 inches (26,461 millimeters) in one year (Cherrapunji, India, 1861).

INTERCEPTION

When precipitation reaches the surface in vegetated areas, a certain percentage of it is retained on or intercepted by the vegetation. Rainfall that is not intercepted is referred to as throughfall. Water that reaches the ground via the trunks and stems of vegetation is called stemflow. The interception storage capacities of vegetation vary with the type and structure of the vegetation and with meteorologic factors. Measurements have shown that up to 0.3 inch (8 millimeters) of rainfall can be intercepted by some vegetation canopies. The intercepted water is evaporated back into the atmosphere at rates determined by the prevailing meteorologic conditions and the nature of the vegetation. In humid temperate areas evaporation of intercepted water can be an important component of the water balance. Forest areas have been shown to have greater interception losses than adjacent grassland areas. This is due to the greater aerodynamic

Hydrologists can help city planners better understand how to handle heavy precipitation to prevent flooding and erosion.

roughness of the forest canopy, resulting in a much more efficient transfer of water vapor away from the surface.

INFILTRATION

When water from a rainstorm or a period of snowmelt reaches the ground, some or all of it will infiltrate the soil. The rate of infiltration depends on the intensity of the input, the initial moisture condition of the surface soil layer, and the hydraulic characteristics of the soil. Small-scale effects such as the presence of a surface seal of low permeability (due to the rearrangement of surface soil particles by rain splash) or the presence of large channels and cracks in the surface soil may be important in controlling infiltration rates. Water in excess of the infiltration capacity of the soil will flow overland as surface runoff once the minor undulations in the surface (the depression storage) have been filled. Such runoff occurs most frequently on bare soils and in areas subject to high rainfall intensities. In many environments rainfall intensities rarely exceed the infiltration capacities of vegetated soil surfaces. The occurrence of surface runoff is then more likely to be generated by rainfall on completely saturated soil.

EVAPOTRANSPIRATION

Evaporation and transpiration are processes that move water to the atmosphere from Earth's surface. Evaporation refers to water that is lost to the atmosphere from bodies of water, such as oceans, lakes, and streams, and also the ground. Transpiration is the movement of water from plants (more specifically, from plant leaves) to the atmosphere. Because both processes result in the net movement of water from Earth's surface to the atmosphere, many hydrologists sum these processes together as evapotranspiration.

Rates of evapotranspiration of water back to the atmosphere depend on the nature of the surface, the availability of water, and the "evaporative demand" of the atmosphere (that is, the rate at which water vapor can be transported away from the surface under the prevailing meteorologic conditions). Estimation of evapotranspiration rates is important in determining expected rates of stream discharge and in controlling irrigation schemes. The concept of potential evapotranspiration—the possible rate of loss without any limits imposed by the supply of water—has been an important one in the development of hydrology. Most

direct measurements of rates of potential evapotranspiration are made using standard evapotranspiration pans with an open water surface. Such measurements serve as a useful standard for comparative purposes, but measured rates may be very different from appropriate potential rates for the surrounding surfaces because of the different thermal and roughness characteristics of the vegetation. In fact, the measured pan rate may be affected by the nature of the surrounding surface due to the influence of evapotranspiration on the humidity of the lower atmosphere.

A distinction also must be drawn between potential rates of evapotranspiration and actual rates. Actual rates may be higher than pan rates for a well-watered, rough vegetation canopy. With a limited water supply available from moisture in the soil, actual rates will fall below potential rates, gradually declining as the moisture supply is depleted. Plants can have some effect on rates of evapotranspiration under dry conditions through physiological controls on their stomata—small openings in the leaf surfaces that are the primary point of transfer of water vapor to the atmosphere. The degree of control varies with plant species.

The only reliable way of measuring actual evapotranspiration is to use large containers called lysimeters, evaluate the different components of the water balance precisely, and calculate the evapotranspiration by subtraction. A similar technique is often employed at the catchment scale, although the measurement of the other components of the water balance is then necessarily less precise.

SOIL MOISTURE

The soil provides a major reservoir for water within a catchment. Soil moisture levels rise when there is sufficient rainfall to exceed losses to evapotranspiration and drainage to streams and groundwater. They are depleted during the summer when evapotranspiration rates are high. Levels of soil moisture are important for plant and crop growth, soil erosion, and slope stability. The moisture status of the soil is expressed in terms of moisture content and the capillary potential of the water held in the soil pores. As the soil becomes wet, the water is held in larger pores, and the capillary potential increases.

Capillary potential may be measured by using a tensiometer consisting of a water-filled porous cup connected to a manometer or pressure transducer. Soil moisture content is often measured gravimetrically by drying a soil

sample under controlled conditions, though there are now available moisture meters based on the scattering of neutrons or absorption of gamma rays from a radioactive source.

The rate at which water flows through soil is dependent on the gradient of hydraulic potential (the sum of capillary potential and elevation) and the physical properties of the soil expressed in terms of a parameter called hydraulic conductivity, which varies with soil moisture in a nonlinear way. Measured sample values of hydraulic conductivity have been shown to vary rapidly in space, making the use of measured point values for predictive purposes at larger scales subject to some uncertainty.

Water also moves in soil because of differences in temperature and chemical concentrations of solutes in soil water. The latter, which can be expressed as an osmotic potential, is particularly important for the movement of water into plant roots due to high solute concentrations within the root water.

GROUNDWATER

Some rocks allow little or no water to flow through; these are known as impermeable

Soil plays a large part in capturing water from precipitation, helping regulate water levels.

rocks, or aquicludes. Others are permeable and allow considerable storage of water, and act as major sources of water supply; these are known as aquifers. Aquifers overlain by an impermeable layer are called confined aquifers; aquifers overlain by an unsaturated, or vadose, zone of permeable materials are called unconfined aquifers. The boundary between the saturated and unsaturated zones is known as the water table. In some confined aquifers, hydraulic potentials may exceed those required to bring the water to the surface. These are artesian aquifers. A well drilled into such an aquifer will cause water to gush to the surface, sometimes with considerable force. Continued use of artesian water, however, will cause potentials to decline until eventually the water may have to be pumped to the surface.

The water found in groundwater bodies is replenished by drainage through the soil, which is often a slow process. This drainage is referred to as groundwater recharge. Rates of groundwater recharge are greatest when rainfall inputs to the soil exceed evapotranspiration losses. When the water table is deep underground, the water of the aquifer may be exceedingly old, possibly resulting from a past climatic regime. A good example is the water of

Impermeable rocks, or aquicludes, such as those that make up Eagle Cliff Falls in Montour Falls, New York, allow little if any water absorption.

the Nubian sandstone aquifer, which extends through several countries in an area that is now the Sahara. The water is being used extensively for water supply and irrigation purposes. Radioisotope dating techniques have shown that this water is many thousands of years old. The use of such water, which is not being recharged under the current climatic regime, is termed groundwater mining.

In many aquifers, groundwater levels have fallen drastically in recent times. Such depletion increases pumping costs, causes wells and rivers to dry up, and, where a coastal aquifer is in hydraulic contact with seawater, can cause the intrusion of saline water. Attempts have been made to augment recharge by the use of waste waters and the ponding of excess river flows. A scheme to pump winter river flows into the Chalk aquifer that underlies London has reversed the downward trend of the water table.

Water table levels in an aquifer are measured by using observation wells. Successive measurements of water levels over time may be plotted as a well hydrograph. The hydraulic characteristics of a particular aquifer around a well can be determined by the response of the water table to controlled pumping. Many aquifers exhibit two types of water storage:

primary porosity consisting of the smaller pores and secondary porosity or fractures within the rock mass. The latter may make up only a small proportion of the total pore space but may dominate the flow characteristics of the aquifer. They are of particular importance to the movement of pollutants through the groundwater.

RUNOFF AND STREAM DISCHARGE

Runoff is the downward movement of surface water under gravity in channels ranging from small streams to large rivers. Channel flows of this sort can be perennial (flowing all the time), or they can be ephemeral (flowing intermittently after periods of rainfall or snowmelt). Such surface waters provide the majority of the water utilized by humans. Some rivers, such as the Colorado River in the western United States, are used so intensively that often no water reaches the sea. Others flowing through hot, dry areas, as, for example, the Lower Nile, become smaller downstream as they lose water to evaporation and groundwater storage.

Stream discharge is normally expressed in units of volume per unit time (for example, cubic meters per second). This is sometimes

converted to an equivalent depth over the upstream catchment area. There are several ways to measure stream discharge. Measurements of velocities using current meters or ultrasonic sounding can be multiplied by the cross-sectional area of flow. Dilution of a tracer can also be used to estimate the total discharge. Weirs (barriers constructed across rivers that affect flow) are frequently employed at discharge measurement sites. The weirs are constructed so as to give a unique relationship between upstream water level and stream discharge. Water levels can then be measured continuously, usually with a float recorder, to construct a record of discharge over time. This is called a stream hydrograph. Analysis of the hydrographic response to catchment inputs can reveal much about the nature of the catchment and the hydrologic processes within it.

Stream discharge data are presented in terms of daily, monthly, and annual flow volumes. For some purposes, such as flood routing, it may be more appropriate to study discharge over shorter time periods.

The frequency characteristics of peak discharges and low flows are also of importance to water resource planning. These are analyzed using some assumed probability distribution in a way similar to rainfalls. A time recording of

When a heavy rainfall occurs, water that does not infiltrate the soil flows over the surface of the ground into streams. This runoff continues moving downward through streams until it reaches the ocean.

annual maximum flood is usually used in flood-frequency analysis. For design purposes the hydrologist may be asked to estimate the flood with a recurrence interval of 50 or 100 years or longer. There are few discharge records that are longer than 50 years, so such estimates are almost always based on inadequate data.

Knowledge of the discharge characteristics of catchments is essential to water supply planning and management, flood forecasting and routing, and floodplain regulation. Discharges vary over short lengths of time during storm periods, seasonally with the seasonal changes in evapotranspiration losses, and over longer periods of time as the rainfall regime changes from year to year.

Discharge characteristics also vary with climate. In some places discharge represents only a minor component of the catchment water balance, the losses being dominated by evapotranspiration.

The discharge hydrograph that results from a rainstorm represents the integrated effects of the surface and subsurface flow processes in the catchment. Traditionally, hydrologists have considered the bulk of a storm hydrograph to consist of storm rainfall that has reached the stream primarily by surface routes. Recent work using naturally occurring isotope tracers such as deuterium has shown, however, that in many humid temperate areas the bulk of the storm hydrograph consists of pre-event water. This water has been stored within the catchment between storms and displaced by the rainfall during the

WATER QUALITY

Natural water is a dilute solution of elements dissolved from Earth's crust or washed from the atmosphere. Its ionic concentration varies from less than 100 milligrams per liter in snow, rain, hail, and some mountain lakes and streams to as high as 400,000 milligrams per liter in the saline lakes of internal drainage systems or old groundwaters associated with marine sediments.

Water quality is influenced by natural factors and by human activities, both of which are the subject of much hydrologic study. The natural quality of water varies from place to place with climate and geology, with stream discharge, and with the season of the year. After precipitation reaches the ground, water percolates through organic material such as roots and leaf litter, dissolves minerals from the soil and rock through which it flows, and reacts with living things from microscopic organisms to humans. Water quality also is modified by temperature, soil bacteria, evaporation, and other environmental factors.

Pollution is the degradation of water quality by human activities. Pollution of surface and subsurface waters arises from many causes, but it is having increasingly serious effects on hydrologic systems. In some areas the precipitation inputs to the system are already highly polluted, primarily by acids resulting from the combustion of fossil fuels in power generation and automobiles.

Other serious causes of pollution have been the dumping of industrial wastes and the discharge of untreated sewage into watercourses. Salt spread on roads in winter has resulted in the contamination of subsurface drinking water supplies in certain areas, as, for example, in Long Island, New York. Excess water resulting from deforestation or irrigation return flows that leach salts from soils in semiarid areas are major sources of pollution in the western United States and western Australia.

storm. This suggests that subsurface flow processes may play a more important role in the storm response of catchments than has previously been thought possible.

RIVERS

A river starts as a tiny trickle, or rill, on a slope. Rainfall, snowfall, a spring, or the melting of glacial ice may be its source. As it flows downhill it is joined by other trickles to make a brook. Other brooks add their waters to form a stream, which broadens into a creek. As the water continues its downward journey, it gains in volume and finally becomes a river.

Along its course, the river receives water from inflowing streams called branches, or tributaries. The river and its branches make up a river system. The area that the system drains is its basin. A divide separates the drainage areas of neighboring streams.

Rivers are also fed by groundwater—water that has soaked into the earth instead of running off the surface. This water flows steadily into the river—sometimes through underground springs.

Nearly all rivers have an upper, middle, and lower course. Each level has its own characteristics. The upper course begins at higher elevations. Here the river is smaller and usually has a rapid, tumbling flow that cuts a narrow channel through rocky hills or mountains. It may roll large boulders along in its swift current.

The river creates waterfalls where it carves out layers of soft rock and leaves a cliff of hard or resistant rock standing. It forms rapids along sloping rocky beds.

When a hard rock formation follows a definite line in a region, all the rivers that cross it there have falls. This is called the fall line. When a river reaches a level or a sunken area, it may form a lake. Over thousands or millions of years the river wears away soil and rocks and carves a canyon or a deep, V-shaped valley. The type of formation it creates depends on the force of the river and the type of material it erodes.

When the river descends to lower elevations, it runs more slowly over the gently sloping land of its middle course. Its current no longer has the force to carry stones or gravel. This material drops to the riverbed, where it forms bars of sand or gravel, or builds islands. These formations are continually changing shape as the river deposits or erodes material. The formations affect the river in turn by altering its course. River currents swing toward one bank

or the other, gradually undercutting the banks and widening a V-shaped valley into a U shape. In the United States, V-shaped valleys are more common in the geologically younger western states while U-shaped valleys are found in the older regions of the central and eastern states.

As the river flows downstream it reaches the still gentler slope of its lower course. It drops more of its load than it did upstream and begins to build up its bed (aggradation) instead of tearing it down (degradation). The valley has been eroded into a wide plain. The river swings in great S-shaped curves, forming loops called meanders.

When a river floods, it may cut across the narrow part of the loop, making a new, shorter channel. The loop is left as a lake known as an oxbow lake. Braided channels appear when the river level falls and exposes bars of sand or gravel. A single meandering channel can become braided downstream from a tight bend in the river, where coarse material is brought up from the river bottom to form sandbars or islands of gravel.

At times heavy rain or melting snow rushes from the upper or middle course of a river into the shallow channel of the lower course. The river floods the surrounding country, leaving a thin layer of sediment. If the flooding is seasonal, in time the layers of sediment accumulate and build a broad, fertile floodplain, like that along the Mississippi and the Nile. Most of the silt and sand drops nearest the channel, forming a broad embankment, or levee. In time the river may flow on a bed higher than the level of the plain. The fertile soil of floodplains attracts human settlement, but flooding can destroy crops and property along the river. To protect the plain, engineers may deepen the channel by dredging accumulated sediment from the riverbed, or they may build artificial levees, or dikes, to contain the river as it rises.

When the river reaches the sea, it deposits its remaining load of silt, gravel, and sand at its mouth. This material builds an ever-growing triangular area called a delta. Here the river branches into several distributaries that empty into the ocean. The mixture of fresh and salt water often gives rise to unique plants and animals. If some distributaries become choked with silt or plant life, the river creates new distributaries and enlarges the delta. Wherever a seacoast has sunk at the mouth of a river, the ocean flows into the river valley, forming an estuary. The mouth of the St. Lawrence River is an estuary.

CHAPTER 6

STUDY OF LAKES

L imnology is concerned with both natural and man-made lakes, their physical characteristics, ecology, chemical characteristics, internal energy fluxes, and exchanges with the environment. It often includes the ecology and biogeochemistry of flowing freshwater. The study of areas that used to be lakes is known as paleolimnology. This science uses inference to study the history of a former lake basin on the basis of evidence contained in the lake-bed sediments.

Lakes may be formed as a result of tectonic activity, glacial activity, volcanism, and by solution of the underlying rock. Man-made lakes or reservoirs may result from the building of a dam within a natural catchment area or as a complete artificial impoundment. In the former case the reservoir may be filled by natural flow from upstream; in the latter the supply of water must be piped or pumped from a surface or subsurface source. The use of reservoir

Lake Tahoe is located in the Sierra Nevada mountain range, on the border of Nevada and California.

water for water supply, river regulation, or hydroelectric power generation may cause rapid changes in water levels that would not normally occur in a natural lake. In addition, water is usually drawn from a reservoir at some depth, resulting in a shorter residence time relative to an equivalent natural lake.

THE HISTORY OF LAKES

A newly formed lake generally contains few nutrients and can sustain only a small amount

of living things and organic matter. Such a lake is described as oligotrophic. Natural processes will supply nutrients to a lake in solution in river water and rainwater, in the fallout of dust from the atmosphere, and in association with the sediments washed into the lake. The lake will gradually become eutrophic, also known as overenriched. The excess of nutrients in a eutrophic lake results in poor water quality but high biological production. Infilling by sediments means that the lake will gradually become shallower; eventually it will disappear.

Natural rates of eutrophication are normally relatively slow. Human activities, however, can greatly accelerate the process by the addition of excessive nutrients in wastewater and the residues of agricultural fertilizers. The result may be excessive biomass production. This is evidenced by phytoplankton "blooms" and the rapid growth of invasive plants such as *Eichhornia*.

The Physical Characteristics of Lakes

The most important physical characteristic of the majority of lakes is their pattern of temperatures—in particular, the changes of

The intensely blue Lake Tahoe took its name from the Washoe Indian word meaning "big water."

temperature with depth. The vertical profile of temperature may be measured using an array of temperature probes. These may be deployed either from a boat or from a stationary platform. Remote-sensing techniques are being used increasingly to observe patterns of temperature and, in particular, to identify the thermal plumes associated with thermal pollution.

In summer the water of many lakes becomes stratified into a warmer upper layer, called the epilimnion, and a cooler lower layer, called the

hypolimnion. The stratification plays a major role in the movement of nutrients and dissolved oxygen and has an important control effect on lake ecology. Between the layers there usually exists a zone of very rapid temperature change known as the thermocline. When the lake begins to cool at the end of summer, the cooler surface water tends to sink because it has greater density. Eventually this results in a mixing of the layers. Temperature change with depth is generally much smaller in winter. Some lakes, called dimictic lakes, can also exhibit a spring overturn following the melting of ice cover since water has a maximum density at 4 °C.

A second important characteristic of lakes is the way that the availability of light changes with depth. Light decreases greatly depending on the turbidity, or cloudiness, of the water. At a point called the compensation depth the light available for photosynthetic production is just matched by the energy lost through cellular respiration. Above the compensation depth is the euphotic zone—the layer that receives sunlight. Below the compensation depth is the aphotic zone, where light does not penetrate. Phytoplankton—the base of the lake food web and thus the support of the entire lake ecosystem—cannot survive in this zone unless the organisms are capable of vertical migration.

Patterns of sediment deposition in lakes depend on the rates of supply in inflowing waters and on subsurface currents and topography. Repetitive sounding of the lake bed may be used to investigate patterns of sedimentation. Remote sensing of the turbidity of the surface waters also has been used to infer rates of sedimentation, as in the artificial Lake Nasser in Egypt. In some parts of the world where erosion rates are high, the operational life of reservoirs may be reduced dramatically by infilling with sediment.

WATER AND ENERGY FLUXES IN LAKES

The water balance of a lake may be evaluated by considering an extended form of the catchment water balance equation outlined in chapter 5, with additional terms for any natural or artificial inflows. An energy balance equation may be defined in a similar way, including terms for the exchange of radiation with the Sun and atmosphere and for the movement of heat through convection and evaporation. Heat also is gained and lost with any inflows and discharges from the lake. The energy

SALTWATER LAKES

Not all lakes contain freshwater. The Dead Sea is a very salty lake that lies in a sunken rift in Israel and Jordan. With a surface 1,316 feet (401 meters) below sea level, it is the lowest lake in the world. Another body of salt water, the Great Salt Lake in Utah, is what remains today of a once much larger freshwater body named Lake Bonneville. The freshwater lake shrank as the climate became drier, and the lake began to evaporate. All the dissolved salts brought in by its tributary rivers were slowly concentrated in less and less water, so each year the water became saltier. This process is still going on. A novel feature of these saltwater lakes is the buoyancy they offer to swimmers: it is much easier to float in the Dead Sea or the Great Salt Lake than in a freshwater lake.

The saline waters of the Dead Sea have a high density that keeps bathers afloat. The lake's extreme salinity excludes all forms of life except bacteria.

balance equation controls the thermal regime of the lake and consequently has an important effect on the ecology of the lake.

Currents play an important role in controlling the distribution of temperature in a lake. These may be due to either the action of the wind blowing across the surface of the lake or the effect of inflows and outflows, especially where a lake receives the cooling water from a power-generation plant.

In large lakes, Earth's rotation has an important effect on the flow of water within the lake. The action of the wind can drive the formation of waves and, when surface water is blown toward a shore, in an accumulation of water that causes a rise in water level called wind setup. In Lake Erie in North America, increases in water level of more than three feet (one meter) have been observed following severe storms. After a storm the water raised in this way causes a seiche (an oscillatory wave of long period) to travel across the lake and back. Seiches are distinctive features of such long, narrow lakes as Switzerland's Lake Zürich, where the wind blows along the axis of the lake. Internal seiche waves can occur in stratified lakes with layers of different density.

THE WATER QUALITY OF LAKES

The biological health of a lake is crucially dependent on its chemical characteristics. Limnologists and hydrobiologists are attentive

Fish can die off in lakes if the water temperature is too high.

to the dissolved oxygen content of the water because it is a primary indicator of water quality. Well-oxygenated water is considered to be of good quality. Low dissolved oxygen content results in anaerobic fermentation. This process, in turn, releases such gases as toxic hydrogen sulfide into the water, with a drastic effect on biological processes.

Another major concern of limnologists and hydrobiologists is the cycling of basic nutrients within a lake system, particularly carbon, nitrogen, phosphorus, and sulfate. An excess of the latter in runoff waters entering a lake may result in high concentrations of hydrogen ions in the water. Hydrogen ions act as weak acids, and thus lower the lake water pH, which is harmful to the lake biology. In particular, aluminium compounds are soluble in water at low pH. The subsequent release of aluminum in the water may cause fish to die because of the damage caused to their gills.

CHAPTER 7

PRACTICAL APPLICATIONS

Water is essential to many of humankind's most basic activities—agriculture, forestry, industry, power generation, and recreation. As the hydrologic sciences provide much of the knowledge and understanding on which the development and management of available water resources are based, they are of fundamental importance.

DEVELOPMENT AND MANAGEMENT OF WATER RESOURCES

In 1965 the United Nations Educational, Scientific and Cultural Organization (UNESCO) initiated the International Hydrological Decade (IHD), a 10-year program that provided an important impetus to international collaboration in hydrology. Considerable progress was made in hydrology during the IHD, but much still remains to be done, both in the basic understanding

Reservoirs are essential in making sure the population has adequate water resources, not only for drinking but also for agriculture and industry.

of hydrologic processes and in the development and conservation of available water resources. Many developing countries remain highly susceptible to diseases related to a lack of water supplies of good quality and to the effects of drought. This was cruelly highlighted by the severe droughts in the Sahel region of Africa in the periods 1969–74 and 1982–85.

In developed countries the ready availability of a supply of good quality water is expected. Yet, even in the most advanced countries, many water sources are not being used wisely.

Groundwater levels in certain areas have fallen dramatically since the 1940s, leading to ever higher pumping costs. Other surface and subsurface water sources are becoming increasingly polluted by urban, agricultural, and industrial wastes in spite of increased expenditure on wastewater treatment and legislation of minimum quality standards. Humankind continues to use the oceans as a vast dumping ground for its waste products, even though little is known about the effects of such wastes on marine ecosystems. It is no exaggeration to say that the misuse of water resources will become a major source of conflict between communities, states, and nations in the years to come. Already several disputes over rights to clean water have taken on international significance.

Since the early 1980s the acid rain problem has assumed scientific, economic, and political prominence in North America and Europe. This major environmental problem serves to illustrate the interdependence of the various hydrologic sciences with other scientific disciplines and human activities. As was noted earlier, waste gases (primarily oxides of sulfur and nitrogen) enter the atmosphere from the burning of fossil fuels by automobiles and electric power plants. These gases combine

Many people in the developed world take the availability of water for granted.

with water vapor in the atmosphere to form sulfuric and nitric acids. When rain or some other form of precipitation falls to Earth, it is highly acidic (often with a pH value of less than 4). The resultant acidification of surface and subsurface waters has been shown to have detrimental effects on the ecology of affected catchments. Areas underlain by slowly weathering bedrock, such as in Scandinavia, the Adirondack Mountains of New York, and the Canadian Shield in Quebec are particularly susceptible. Many lakes in these areas have been shown to be biologically dead. There also is evidence that the growth of trees may be affected, with consequent economic ramifications where forestry is a major activity. The areas most greatly affected may be far downwind of the source of the pollution. A number of countries have claimed that the major sources of acid rain affecting their streams and lakes lie outside their borders.

Research has revealed that in an area susceptible to the effects of acid rain short-lived events can have a particularly damaging effect. These "acid shocks" may be due to inputs of highly acidic water from a single storm or to the first snowmelt outflows in which the major part of the pollutant input accumulated over the winter is concentrated. The way in which the chemistry of the input water is modified in its flow through the catchment depends both on the nature of the soils and rocks in

CAREERS IN OCEANOGRAPHY

There are many opportunities for employment in the general field of oceanography through research organizations and industrial firms that have interests in the ocean. A research oceanographer usually has a bachelor's degree with studies in the basic sciences of physics, chemistry, and biology and

CONTINUED ON THE NEXT PAGE

CONTINUED FROM PAGE 113

often with specialized postgraduate training. The field of oceanography is traditionally divided into four major areas of research: physical, chemical, biological, and geological. Increased use of ocean resources has fostered new branches that deal with public policy, archaeology, conservation, and many environmental concerns.

Physical oceanographers describe the physical state of the sea, particularly the distribution of water masses, the conditions that form them, and the great currents that disperse and mix them. Chemical oceanographers study the chemical constituents of seawater and their consequences on biological, geological, and physical processes in the marine environment. Biological oceanographers study the plants, animals, and other organisms that live in the sea. Geological oceanographers are concerned with the geological structure and mineral content of the ocean floor as well as with phenomena ranging in scale from the planetary to that of individual sediment particles.

Increased opportunities and uses of the ocean have created needs for public policies, such as an international law of the sea. Marine archaeologists study submerged artifacts, often attempting to reconstruct seacoast habitats of the past. Studies of the wreck of the *Nuestra Señora de Atocha* off Key West, Florida, one of the richest and most profitable archaeological treasure finds of all time, and of the site of the *Titanic* are notable achievements.

A research diver deploys a self-contained instrument package.

the catchment and on the flow paths taken through the system. These interactions are at present poorly understood. It is likely, however, that the attempt to understand the chemical processes within the different flow paths will lead to significant improvements in scientific understanding of catchment hydrology.

CONCERN OVER GROUNDWATER QUANTITY AND QUALITY

Groundwater problems are becoming increasingly serious in many areas of the world. Rapid increases in the rates of pumping of groundwater in many aquifers has caused a steady lowering of water table levels where extraction has exceeded rates of recharge. A notable example is the Ogallala aquifer, a sandy formation some 330 feet (100 meters) thick, which lies beneath the Great Plains from South Dakota to Texas. It has been estimated that as much as 60 percent of the total storage of this huge aquifer has already been extracted primarily for agricultural use. The remaining water, if it continues to be mined in this way, will become more and more expensive to extract. This situation points out the importance of

understanding groundwater flow and recharge processes in complex heterogeneous formations so that safe yields of aquifers can be properly predicted.

There are many causes of groundwater pollution; most are the accidental or incidental consequences of human activities. In some cases, however, groundwater may be contaminated because of planned human effort. Subsurface repositories of water, for example, have been considered as possible receptacles for waste products, including radioactive materials. This has resulted in both experimental and model studies of water flows in poorly permeable massive rocks that would be used to store such wastes. The effects of joints and fractures on the very slow transport of contaminants over long periods of time in such rocks is as yet uncertain but must be clarified if this form of storage is to be proved safe.

STUDYING THE CAUSES OF DROUGHTS AND OTHER CLIMATIC PATTERNS

Another subject still poorly understood is the occurrence of droughts in areas of highly variable rainfall. In the early 1970s and again in the

Since water is essential to life, drought can have a lasting negative impact on communities.

early 1980s the Sahel region of Africa suffered periods of severe drought, resulting in wide-spread famine and death. The consequences of

these droughts were exacerbated by increased populations of people and grazing animals. The combination of drought and population growth results in desertification. It remains an unanswered scientific question as to whether the deterioration of the Sahel and other marginal lands is part of a long-term natural change or whether it is a result of human activities.

Some evidence for long-range interactions in the occurrence of droughts and other climatic regimes comes from studies of the ocean currents. It is known that the oceans are a major controlling influence on climate, but the processes involved remain the subject of active research. Some clues have been revealed by studies of El Niño, a minor branch of the Pacific Equatorial Countercurrent that flows south along the coasts of Colombia and Ecuador, where it meets the northward-flowing Peru Current. The cold Peru Current keeps rainfall along the coastal area of Peru very low but maintains a rich marine life, which in turn supports major bird populations and a fishing industry. In certain years El Niño becomes much stronger, forcing the Peru Current to the south. Storms rake the coast, causing flooding and erosion. The sudden change in sea temperatures causes dramatic decreases in plankton production and, consequently, in fish and bird populations.

Catastrophic El Niño events occurred in 1925, 1933, 1939, 1944, 1958, 1983, and 1998. This last event is regarded by some scientists as the strongest such event of the 20th century, producing drought conditions in Brazil, Indonesia, Malaysia, and the Philippines and bringing heavy rains to the dry seacoast of Peru. In the United States the southeastern states and California experienced significant increases in winter rainfall, and record-breaking warm temperatures in the upper Midwest caused some journalists to label the period "the year without a winter."

Explanations of the El Niño events have invoked both local and long-range interactions in the circulation of the Pacific winds and currents. The study of such dramatic events, enhanced by remote sensing and computer modeling, is a major stimulus to understanding the general circulation of Earth's atmosphere and oceans.

CONCLUSION

Water is the most abundant substance on Earth and is the principal constituent of all living things. Water in the atmosphere plays a major role in maintaining a habitable environment for human life. The occurrence of surface waters has played a significant role in the rise and decline of the major civilizations in world history. In many societies the importance of water to humankind is reflected in the legal and political structures. At the present time, rising populations and improving living standards are placing increasing pressures on available water resources. There is, in general, no shortage of water on Earth's land surface, but areas of surplus water are often located far from major centers of population. Moreover, in many cases these centers prove to be sources of water pollution. Thus, the availability and quality of water are becoming an ever-increasing constraint on human activities, notwithstanding the great technological advances that have been made in the control of surface waters. As a result, the studies of oceanography and hydrology are more important than ever.

basin A large or small depression in the surface of the land or in the ocean floor.

bedrock The solid rock underlying unconsolidated surface materials (as soil).

catchment In hydrology, an area that catches or collects water draining from rivers and streams; also called a watershed.

chloride A compound of chlorine with another element or group.

climatic Of or relating to climate.

continent One of Earth's great divisions of land, namely, Asia, Africa, North America, South America, Antarctica, Europe, and Australia.

convection Movement in a gas or liquid in which the warmer parts move up and the colder parts move down.

density The mass of a substance per unit volume.

ecology A branch of science concerned with the interrelationship of organisms and their environments; or, the relationships between a group of living things and their environment.

equator An imaginary circle around Earth

everywhere equally distant from the North Pole and the South Pole.

erosion The transport of materials such as sediment and rock by natural forces.

evaporation The process of changing from a liquid into a gas.

geology A science that studies rocks, minerals, soil, and other aspects of the solid Earth.

glacier A very large area of ice that moves slowly down a slope or valley or over a wide area of land.

Gulf Stream Warm current in the North Atlantic Ocean flowing from the Gulf of Mexico northeast along the U.S. coast to Nantucket and then eastward toward northern Europe.

hemisphere A half of Earth.

hydrology A science dealing with the properties, distribution, and circulation of water on and below Earth's surface and in the atmosphere.

hydrosphere The part of Earth that includes all the liquid water on, just below, and just above the surface.

impermeable Not permitting passage (as of a fluid) through its substance.

iron oxide A chemical compound containing iron and oxygen.

landlocked Enclosed or nearly enclosed by land.

marine Of or relating to the sea or the plants and animals that live in the sea.

meteorology A science that deals with the atmosphere and with weather.

oceanography A science dealing with all aspects of the oceans, including their physical and chemical properties, their geology, and their life forms.

American Ground Water Trust
50 Pleasant Street
Concord, NH 03301
(603) 228-5444
Website: www.agwt.org
The American Ground Water Trust communicates the environmental and economic value of groundwater and promotes efficient and effective groundwater management.

American Institute of Hydrology
Engineering D - Mail Code 6603
Southern Illinois University Carbondale
1230 Lincoln Drive
Carbondale, IL 62901
(618) 453-7809
Website: http://www.aihydrology.org
The American Institute of Hydrology is the only nationwide organization that offers certification to qualified professionals in all fields of the hydrological sciences.

American Water Resources Association
P.O. Box 1626
Middleburg, VA 20118

(540) 687-8390
Website: www.awra.org
The goal of the American Water Resources
    Association is to educate the public
    about water resources and related issues.

Canadian Meteorological and
    Oceanographic Society
P.O. Box 3211
Station D
Ottawa, ON K1P 6H7
Canada
(613) 990-0300
Website: www.cmos.ca
The Canadian Meteorological and
    Oceanographic Society is dedicated
    to advancing atmospheric and oceanic
    sciences and related environmental disci-
    plines in Canada.

Consortium for Ocean Leadership
1201 New York Avenue NW, 4th Floor
Washington, D.C. 20005
(202) 232-3900
Website: www.oceanleadership.org
The Consortium for Ocean Leadership
    is a nonprofit organization located in
    Washington, D.C., that represents more

than 100 of the leading public and private ocean research and educational institutions. Its mission is to advance research, education, and sound ocean policy.

Woods Hole Oceanographic Institution
266 Woods Hole Road
Woods Hole, MA 02543-1050
(508) 289-2252
Website: www.whoi.edu
The Woods Hole Oceanographic Institution is dedicated to advancing the understanding of the ocean and its interaction with the Earth system.

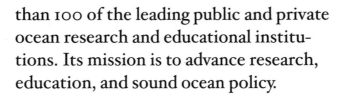

WEBSITES

Because of the changing nature of Internet links, Rosen Publishing has developed an online list of websites related to the subject of this book. This site is updated regularly. Please use this link to access the list:

http://www.rosenlinks.com/SCI/Ocean

FOR FURTHER READING

Anderson, Michael, ed. *Investigating Earth's Oceans*. New York, NY: Britannica Educational Publishing, 2012.

Cousteau, Fabien. *Ocean: The Definitive Visual Guide*. Revised ed. New York, NY: Dorling Kindersley, 2014.

Earle, Sylvia A. *Blue Hope: Exploring and Caring for Earth's Magnificent Ocean*. Washington, DC: National Geographic, 2014.

Fishman, Charles. *The Big Thirst: The Secret Life and Turbulent Future of Water*. New York, NY: Free Press, 2011.

Green, Jen. *Rivers Around the World*. New York, NY: PowerKids Press, 2009.

Kareiva, Peter M., and Michelle Marvier. *Conservation Science: Balancing the Needs of People and Nature*. 2nd ed. Greenwood Village, CO: Roberts, 2015.

Petersen, Christine. *Renewing Earth's Waters*. New York, NY: Marshall Cavendish Benchmark, 2011.

Rafferty, John P., ed. *Lakes and Wetlands*. New York, NY: Britannica Educational Publishing, 2011.

Rafferty, John P., ed. *Oceans and Oceanography*. New York, NY: Britannica Educational Publishing, 2011.

Rafferty, John P., ed. *Rivers and Streams*. New York, NY: Britannica Educational Publishing, 2011.

Rose, Paul, and Anne Laking. *Oceans: Exploring the Hidden Depths of the Underwater World*. Berkeley, CA: University of California Press, 2009.

Sedlak, David. *Water 4.0*. New Haven, CT: Yale University Press, 2015.